Dear John, Dear Coltrane

POETRY FROM ILLINOIS

A list of books in this series appears at the end of this book.

Books by Michael S. Harper

Healing Song for the Inner Ear
Chant of Saints: A Gathering of Afro-American
    Literature, Art, and Scholarship *(co-editor)*
Images of Kin
Nightmare Begins Responsibility
Debridement
Song: I Want a Witness
Photographs: Negatives: History as Apple Tree
History Is Your Own Heartbeat
Dear John, Dear Coltrane
Heartblow: Black Veils *(editor)*

Dear John, Dear Coltrane

Poems by MICHAEL S. HARPER

University of Illinois Press

Urbana and Chicago

First Illinois paperback edition, 1985
© 1970 by Michael S. Harper
Manufactured in the United States of America
P 9 8 7 6

This book is printed on acid-free paper.

This book was originally published as part of the Pitt Poetry Series
by the University of Pittsburgh Press.

Acknowledgment is made to the following publications in which some of
these poems first appeared: *Burning Deck, Carolina Quarterly, December,
Midwestern University Quarterly, Poetry Northwest, Quarterly Review of
Literature, Southern Review,* and *Sunday Oregonian* (Portland).

"Effendi" and "Malcolm's Blues" were first published in *Negro Digest,*
copyright © 1968, 1969 by *Negro Digest.* Reprinted by permission.

"New Season," "Village Blues," "For Bud," "Savage," "The Black Angel,"
and "Blues Alabama" were first published in *Poetry,* copyright 1968 by The
Modern Poetry Association. Reprinted by permission.

Library of Congress Cataloging in Publication Data

Harper, Michael S., 1938-
    Dear John, dear Coltrane.

    (Poetry from Illinois)
    Reprint. Originally published: Pittsburgh: University of Pittsburgh
Press, 1970.
    I. Title. II. Series.
PS3558.A6248D4   1985   811'.54   84-24149
ISBN 0-252-01193-7 (alk. paper) [previously ISBN 0-8229-3196-6 (cloth);
0-8229-5213-0 (paper)]

For Shirl, who blossomed before my eyes and took me in

CONTENTS

Dear John, Dear Coltrane

BROTHER JOHN

Black man:
I'm a black man;
I'm black; I am—
A black man; black—
I'm a black man;
I'm a black man;
I'm a man; black—
I am—

Bird, buttermilk bird—
smack, booze and bitches
I am Bird
baddest nightdreamer
on sax in the ornithology-world
I can fly—higher, high, higher—
I'm a black man;
I am; I'm a black man—

Miles, blue haze,
Miles high, another bird,
more Miles, mute,
Mute Miles, clean,
bug-eyed, unspeakable,
Miles, sweet Mute,
sweat Miles, black Miles;
I'm a black man;
I'm black; I am;
I'm a black man—

Trane, Coltrane; John Coltrane;
it's tranetime; chase the Trane;
it's a slow dance;

3

it's the Trane
in Alabama; acknowledgement,
a love supreme,
it's black Trane; black;
I'm a black man; I'm black;
I am; I'm a black man—

Brother John, Brother John
plays no instrument;
he's a black man; black;
he's a black man; he is
Brother John; Brother John—

I'm a black man; I am;
black; I am; I'm a black
man; I am; I am;
I'm a black man;
I'm a black man;
I am; I'm a black man;
I am:

for John O. Stewart

4

ALONE

A friend told me
He'd risen above jazz.
I leave him there.

for Miles Davis

WHERE IS MY WOMAN NOW: *For Billie Holiday*

poplars lean backward
greener and sparser
on windward side
where is my woman now
caught in northern spit
losing the weak leaves
and winter bark
the rains till the hillside
while the poppies mope
where is my woman now
on the slopes are sparrows
bathing like sheep
in this spring muck
where is my woman now

LADY'S BLUES

We visit bark
an unmarked grave,
the money
the grass, the ground
your face,
no stone your voice;
we kiss the air.

The chestnut colt
appreciates the green;
never overwhelmed
by its scarcity,
the peaks are rigidly brown.
Occasional horses,
some lying down,
escape gully wind,
sound, and seep the sun
sorting their coats:
bitterness is no more than the weather.
The trucks linger on the summits
like cattle gasping in the distance;
you, a thousand miles westward,
are human, woman, sometimes mine.

VILLAGE BLUES

(After a Story by John O. Stewart)

The birds flit
in the blue palms,
the cane workers wait,
the man hangs
twenty feet above;
he must come down;
they wait for the priest.
The flies ride on the carcass
which sways like cork in a circle.
The easter light pulls him west.
The priest comes, a man
sunken with rum,
his face sandpapered
into a rouge of split
and broken capillaries.
His duty is the cutting
down of this fruit
of this quiet village
and he staggers slowly, coming.

LETTER TO A MOON CHILD

Moon child:
March is coming,
In mixed anger,
To an eventual end.
The trees have cracked
Under the weight of ice,
Blotting power lines,
And we have been without light,
Days, nights, together.
Elms are first to bloom,
Slowly, in fear of constant
Virus, that, heedless,
Will kill them off in ten years;
This year they bloom.
The spindly trees,
Taking shape, resist
The inlet, hornet,
And salt-night air.
In this ribald quiet,
Revisited without shame,
There is evidence,
Ornate, and our hunger.

THE FIREPLACE

Fixed in the fireplace,
gaslit, square with brick
lining the iron frame,
the smashed remains of your
poignant replica remains.
I have killed you I say,
dead, you are without breath.
In its enclosure the flames
eat at the edges of your face,
hot lice infecting the outer
walls, old potato face—
Now, burned up ash
is the last kennel.
Like a dog I eat the soft
remains which blacken
my tongue, and leaving grit,
pleases the image of the flames
breathing restlessly through
gas jets out into the room:
its magic asphyxiates the hall,
and with the smell
consumes your name.

11

ELVIN'S BLUES

Sniffed, dilating my nostrils,
the cocaine creeps up my
leg, smacks into my groin;
naked with a bone for luck,
I linger in stickiness,
tickled in the joints;
I will always be high—

Tired of fresh air,
the stone ground bread,
the humid chant of music
which has led me here,
I reed my song:

"They called me the black
narcissus as I devoured
'the white hopes'
crippled in their inarticulate
madness,
Crippled myself,
Drums, each like porcelain
chamber pots, upside down,
I hear a faggot insult my
white wife with a sexless grin,
maggots under his eyelids,
a candle of my fistprint
breaks the membrane of his nose.
Now he stutters."

Last Thursday, I lay with you
tincturing your womb
with aimless strokes I could not feel.

12

Swollen and hard the weekend,
penitent, inane
I sank into your folds,
or salved your pastel tits,
but could not come.

Sexless as a pimp
dying in performance
like a flare gone down,
the tooth of your pier
hones near the wharf.
The ocean is breathing,
its cautious insomnia—
driven here and there—
with only itself to love.

for Elvin Jones

THE WATERBOWL

Because she had ceased
to cry,
and her eyes had
turned the color
of okra, I took
her pock-boned jaws,
and kissed her lids.

Like a mussel
clamped into darkness
her eyes two matchsticks
in a waterbowl,
soggy with blackness,
there is no love
in those eyes,
only loss, pregnant
with intelligent shame.

THE MOON CHILD

Wretched, outside of Denver,
the mountain road, US 40,
sings snakelike,
in gravelled need of repair.
The skiers are gone,
but fresh snow covers
the firs, in punishment;
the falling rocks cannot slide.
The air is blue at the crest,
smoking, as if bewildered,
and the birches, grey,
file to survive.
It is a game I cannot master.

From her writing
I infuse two months
of imprecise bleeding,
flattening hips,
womb sutured,
the makeup gone
or going;

I read of Minnesota
when she swam
naked with her sisters,
and it rained on her wet hair;
or when the wind blew pollen
into her horse's ears:
She raced the trail-
bats hidden in the elms.

And it is Minnesota
in the rain
with her swimming,
racing the drops,
with her sisters' nude
angles matting their hair;

it is summer on that horse,
the pollen diving in the wind
sticking to her shoulder blades,
fading in her lake,
oily dark with fetus:

and her writing
is smeared over
seventeen years
and her loving
carnivorous family.

FOR BUD

Could it be, Bud
that in slow galvanized
fingers beauty seeped
into *bop* like Bird
weed and Diz clowned—
Sugar waltzing
back into dynamite,
sweetest left hook you
ever dug, baby;
could it violate violence
Bud, like Leadbelly's
chaingang chuckle,
the candied yam
twelve string clutch
of all blues:
there's no rain
anywhere, soft
enough for you.

for Bud Powell

WINTER RETREAT

The trail behind me
Narrows to a point
Where I watched the gulls
Crack the crusty crabs
From great heights,
To feed long among
The pinchers and false eyes.
In winter the seals
Come from New Brunswick
To rest in the inlet,
In fear of the safety they
Know enough to dread;
But they were fed
From the bridge which
Goes to the air base,
And like soldiers
Obeyed their instincts,
And fled; two days
Before the river turned
To ice, locked us,
The boats, and inlet in.

for L&J Inada

SHIRL'S DREAM

No match in the house;
rain belts the windows;
the door jams with sediment;
ants race out;
and you're nine thousand feet
near the sea in Mexico.
The glaze from the clouds
around your pursed shoulders,
and the juarachas on your feet,
are worn from the plateau rock.
In the glue photo, the sky's blue
twin veins on your ankle,
and the fire heats the wind
between us as sure as I see smoke
from under that Indian blanket you're weaving.

CRISIS IN THE MIDLANDS: ST. LOUIS, MISSOURI

Stymied in my leave-taking
I ponder the two vacant days
I have spent in this river town;
My first impression was its cold
Resemblance to Cleveland,
Where through crowded districts,
Blocks of empty lots crowd
The crowded into the old
Slave quarters.
Weary with its dankness,
The slow ebullient waters,
Bland, the pinched
Houses, abandoned
Flights from disaster, I harbour
That festered wound
Internal, and the silence
Of each poisoned day's burning.

THE GATE

More real than the weak
Passing of your sigh,
I peer in some hope of quiet.
The light is disappearing,
And my eyes adjust
To the traffic, dense
In the craze of its motion.
As it grows darker,
I am lost in the mechanics
Of its encroachment.
Were I able
I would not hold it back.
Woman, you claim
You are open
To the challenge I offer,
That night is as black as
Your darkest, grand desire,
And that you sing
In a singular hope
That I am your consummation.

MAINE LANDING

Never before,
And twice in one week,
I have gazed out
Into the oblivion and anger,
Sonorous and punctual,
Of the nearby air base.
They are burning excess
Fuel, with the rigor
Of marksmen;
The elms are dying out
From some virulent virus;
Though it is mid-March
The snow has receded,
And come again,
And there is nothing
In the wind; no music.

Woman with the mirror laugh,
You with the perfect correction
for the ringing magic
of our nutmeg reflection,
when you are bathed,
rinsed in juice from my sight;
is there not a sound of wings
flailing in orbit
of our fingered, paining love,
and is our flight
not long, high, and distant.

ECHOES: TWO

For five hours the two dents
of your face will not disappear.
I feel the shape of your head,
the dark covering, the fine lines
that blister the neck;
and your smile is a haven for those lines.
To love is to memorize the one loved,
to hold in fear the moment
of that memory, to forget
nothing of that memory
whose details are lost.

ECHOES: THREE

Blowing my nose to make it bleed,
four sleepless nights
since you packed
two straw saddle bags
filled with sewing,
my valise, those tired
eyes, pigtailed
into two smiles,
I've picked spattered dust
from your hairs
on these bloodstained floors.
The fifth night I sleep
among your clothes in our closet
but do not dream
for fear you'll not come back;
smelling you everywhere
but where you are.

LOOKOUT POINT: USS SAN FRANCISCO

The gale winds
ripen the cheeks
which splice broken
blood vessels
and force the retreat
to their cars.
The idlers gaze
in agitation
taunting each bridge suicide
from his ecstatic perch:
and the idlers are many.
From Tiburon,
San Quentin,
Poughkeepsie,
from the plains
of our mutual despair;
their love is the hidden
displacement of fear,
and they ride, softly,
weaving in the wind
which drives each down
to the waters below.

DISCOVERY

We lay together, darkness all around,
I listen to her constant breath,
and when I thought she slept,
I too fell asleep.
But something stirred me, why I . . .
she was staring at me with her eyes,
her breasts still sturdy,
her thigh warming mine.
And I, a little shaken as she stroked
my skin and kissed my brow,
reached for the light turned on,
feeling for the heat which would
reveal how long she had looked
and cared.
The bulb was hot.   It burned my hand.

THE BLACK ANGEL

Childhood games,
played without innocence,
and in place of the angel,
take me to a grove of pepper trees;
they lighten my head.
Trees emit their odors,
a natural oxygen tent;
have you noticed the air is heavy
in trees that shed their leaves
without hesitance,
and flow with sap,
and are closest
to the angel's skin;
the eyes, each singly
wide, smarting, unreadable
as the sap, and which
recount the games,
verses, puzzles of other men:
I am reading poems
to this black angel.
Kindled in the shrill
eloquence of other men,
the angel forces open my hands
and in the palms
leaves her footprints.

WELCOME

Spooned in African
food, the moon
sucks vegetable
orchids in what
anthropology
calls—the useless
curiosity.

Now tenor kiss
"Welcome"
tenor love—
the parasite flower
has flourished,
in wounded dancing,
with astounding
equatorial
eloquence.

When the moon's
scientists excavate
these puritan
paranoid scars
black feathered
jazz
will again speak
its loving entreaty:
"Welcome", finally.

for Roland W. Harper

AT THE CUT-OFF: BAY BRIDGE, SAN FRANCISCO

I look at the water's
surface and know no
longing; the channels—
beautiful in purple—
are six brothers who shock
their world with their persistent
breathing, and like magicians
exchange identities;
it is their sounds,
their voices
bending upwards.

THREE O'CLOCK LOVE SONG

Our park empty,
whipped of customers,
the wind, smacked leaves,
grasslips pulled
to the city.
Lull is clear blue
San Francisco
channel water off Point Lobos.
We have photographed this,
with ourselves stuck
into that blue gas
spumed in.
Language is no obstacle;
there is none.
I look at your pumped
flesh and scream
into the form
for love I've put there.
Nerves once pushed
fingernails and skin
from those hands
in answer to cries
no one heard;
cannot be pictured;
sleep you'd lost;
gain; fragment dreams
better than life—
more tragic, more terrible—

are not here.
The vocabulary
of love is silence,
also pictured
in our swirl.

for Shirl

FOOL'S GETAWAY

All over the road
the no-winged geese swim in beams,
their wings whipping the fog;
the fog, the snow, the beams
disappear and birches
grow straight up in clearings
each in cottoned silence.
Because it is my first time
in Oregon, I believe
the eleven o'clock air
is not flooded with animals,
that the animals do not
claim my wife beside me,
that the life she hovers
over is animal also,
beating and clutching
in those trees right there.

THE SKIERS

They are up
on the slopes
broken legs
and scenery
goggles, ski
poles, brandied
menageries
of loss.
They are our
loved ones
in this silk
screen; the 8-
lane roads up
there, concrete,
in and out
arteries
from cities
filled with blacks
everyone's
heard of in
what was once
theirs—they're back
in the snows
where they came
yesterday,
leaving their
tracks, breaking
their legs in
the stampede,
smiling,
understanding all.

CLARK'S WAY WEST: ANOTHER VERSION

The venereal moon
draws six women
to the Missouri River
where they empty their
beaver pelt children
in great Montana falls
near Indian prairie slope.
From the rattler's rattle
their labor was eased
and the children came
from their collective blindness
to the Shawnee burial ground:
each child is blind.
The earth is not invalid here,
the grizzly slaps at salmon,
and stops, and retreats;
and the children bob
down the falls to the basin below.

LETTER FROM A TRAVELER

The car sways at
eighty miles an hour;
the road slants down
from the center,
a banked track,
between Montreal
and the Canadian border.
A black pigeon is caught
in the spokes of the grillwork,
and with his parting feathers,
dies there; slowly he ferments,
sweeter than the windshield insects.
I had expected great
tundra changes,
leaves greener, fat,
the trees shedding
to a purer sky
in its blankness.
It is so much the same.
Customs, and their searching,
has not stung this dream;
the miles I put between us
are simply Canadian miles,
foreign and familiar,
and no distance at all.

for Frances

MALCOLM'S BLUES

So now we have come
to silence
like an ant-race
in a hidden pimple
while in white America
they squeal with
pleasure and assurance
that you've got your kite
caught in a poplar tree:
it doesn't count.

In Chicago
they commemorate
the slums to your
platform,
and the handkerchief
women weep, and
the guns come out
for the thousandth time.
With the revenge
we watch our admissions
of guilt
sink with the shaft of the wasp,
to kiss the white queen—
ass, nose and elbow.

NIGHTDREAMER

She dreams string
after string of episodes;
chalk images stir her eyelids;
tears wind into a small lake,
two lakes, on either side
of her mouth, two smile dents;
the lakes remind me of her birth
in Minnesota.
She's told me of her childhood,
the strange continuum
of her childhood without demons;
her family are the carnivores,
her gnashing teeth
of internal rage,
grey-green, behind her eyes.

Awake now, tired,
she asks about her performance
and is told nothing
of that life that rides within.

SAVAGE

The savage broke the walls out
and bulled into the wilderness.
We sat recalling his unspeakable
ingratitude, of our equipment,
the time we'd lose,
the experiment not yet done.

THE GUERRILLA-CONG

He looks back at me
from LIFE—
Geronimo run down
by black cavalry
in Mexico,
an illiterate Eskimo woman
called Kim,
Charlie Cong;
he looks like a child,
which he is,
though he isn't;
he has fought
361 battles over three years;
He is on CBS
having lost his identity
having lost his genitals
having lost our war.

REMEMBER MEXICO

Villages of high quality
merchandise—hand tooled leather,
blown glass like diamonds,
cloth finer than linen,
delicious food without dysentery,
mountain water from palapa groves
cured by glistening rocks,
burro-drawn carts for the day,
fishing boats destined for clear
water and giant marlin;
the peasants clean
tanned and bilingual;
lemon, papaya,
horseback or raft,
turtle in the picnic
baskets, white lunch
on hacienda siesta—
pure and unblemished
in the public notices.

I remember the birds
of the desert
ripping a horse
not yet fallen;
hookworm, beetles,
the soup of the desert;
cows and donkeys
eat around the cracked
and broken American
automobiles; in this covey
of linkage, spoken here,
I think of Montezuma's

unspeakable rites
in honed rock graves—
bloodmeal and black tunnels;
Indians who speak no Spanish
and worship the sea,
fruit unpicked in suspect
sweetness for corn,
deisel smoke forcing
Indian, and Indian
and Indian, and Indian
farther up the mountainside.

for Carlos Amador

We stand pinned
to the electric mural
of Mexican history
and listen to a paid guide
explain fresco technique
and the vision of Diego Rivera:
Cortes, crippled with disease,
his Indian woman and son,
sailor raping an Indian
in frocks of priesthood.

In the center the Mexican
eagle peels the serpent
and cools his thirst on desert cactus;
Hidalgo forced into Independence,
that bald creole iconoclast
lost east of Guadalajara;
near him, Montezuma
passively meets Cortes,
salutes the Gods,
dies, the mistake of his people;
corn mixes with chickens and goats,
housepets, muskets and cactus wine.

To your left Rockefeller,
Morgan, the atomic bomb,
Wall Street, the pipeline to the Vatican;
below, the Mexican people pay
for the chosen friar
and the dignity of retreat
to the hills above the central valley.

Then comes Juarez—our guide's
voice rings with full-blooded pride
at the full-blooded Indian
busting the military;
he disbands the church,
opens his arms, and gives
the land to the people.
Our guide is speaking in Spanish:
"You see, my friends, we want the land
that Santa Anna gave you for ten
million pesos; we want Texas, Arizona
and the rest of the west;
take the painting, absorb it—
then give us back our land."

EFFENDI

The piano hums
again the clear
story of our coming,
enchained, severed,
our tongues gone,
herds the quiet
musings of ten million
years blackening the earth
with blood and our moon women,
children we loved,
the jungle swept up
in our rhapsodic song
giving back
banana leaves and
the incessant beating
of our tom-tom hearts.
We have sung a long time here
with the cross and the cotton field.
Those white faces turned
away from their mythical
beginnings are no art
but that of violence—
the kiss of death.
Somewhere on the inside
of those faces
are the real muscles
of the world;
the ones strengthened
in experience and pain,
the ones wished for in one's lover

or in the mirror
near the eyes
that record this lost, dogged data
and is pure, new, even lovely
and is you.

for McCoy Tyner

RHAPSODY: OURS

This is the paradise of policemen
the last posse,
the last manhunt,
where the caged Negro children
screech, "Kill me, Kill me,
Kill me,"
in our rhapsody.

NEGRO DEPOT

Welfare workers storm black
uncouth children
and their sexual parents.
Somehow the Negroes increase
the Mississippi basin
plantation, the northern star—
somehow they are here.
Raffle: Dark Bay Horse, "Star",
Mulatto Girl, "Sarah",
each for one hundred dollars,
twenty year old, bred
free of smallpox and scurvy;
utmost care taken with choice
cargo of 250 fine healthy
Negroes—to be sold on board ship.

Can't teach horses or
niggers new tricks, Uncle Sam,
so pay 'em.

THE WHITE WHALE

The gentleman white killer whale
spawns again into the Pacific waters,
spawns the lead-boots and whalebone
kiss of another harbor:
can't somebody teach him how
to love
and bury his oil 'fore
he poisons everybody
with his lead-pipe sperm?

DIRGE FOR TRANE

Gone, gone, gone, gone, gone—
Dead ten days 'fore I knew you dead
the onyx museums
of Mexico, eight thousand
feet between the valleys,
we hear the sinewed vultures
whip those airborne rhythms
of leatherwork and grinding corn.
It is there, at home,
each moment fell into place
and your kiss sprung out
the unbrung melody
killed in your brain,
the canvas soul.

We are alive in the lift
into the plateau region;
bells ring there;
the twelve thousand
missions of the Spanish
friars are not the Yaqui
Indian woman chanting
the ancient *gone*
gone, gone, gone,
gone, gone, gone.

Was it you in Detroit,
Iowa, Spain
caught up in spirals
so exquisite and edible
why would one want
to digest it
into poems, sons,
a faithful woman,
a few tributes
to what you were;
it was the gears
or is
the Spanish wine fillers,
the man with a gun;

it was you in Berenda
Slough, America,
and on a cycle
pumping the rubber
avocado handles
and the lone ring
of all these nectars
tasting the buds.

And Detroit burned—
in Iowa the students
are demonstrating
or so it was
when farm equipment
and corn were there
with the marvelous pigs
five hundred pounds a piece.

In Spain were the Moors—
and the Spanish Civil War,
each without definition;
in America you have
three sons and a woman
and the metaphors
of all this
colliding and colliding
in dissonant music
someone's said
is a symphony:
reds, brown, blacks
all humming
the same old tune:
love me,
love me painlessly—
but you can't.

for Philip Levine

TO JAMES BROWN

Little brother, little brother,
put your feet on the floor.

You've asked for Jimmy Brown,
beautiful cat, the wrong man.

Little brother, don't nobody know
your name, feet off the floor,

movin' again. Black Brother!
Somebody tell little brother

'bout James Brown:
please, please, please,

please, please, please.

AT BEAR MOUNTAIN

He threads his pink paws
on the landing
between floors
a strange bear
with Finnish eyes
and a smooth northern
stiffening of a non-
western man, weaving a'crouch.
He sees in heavy lumps,
his mind sour from losses
he won't calculate
or write into his poems
or speak to his wife,
though they are marked
on steps to this attic-study,
in the railings stacked
with invisible shelves
cancerous as his parents
who've left him speechless
in rage at their leaving;
or the same books
his first son rakes
through for printed
songs on his own lips,
unuttered.

Now I live in the bear's house,
marking the spare implements
he's used, with intense impunity,
a correspondence 'tween
love—loss and family
sleek with warm etchings

of their blossoming:
four bedrooms, an old oil
furnace, the duffled
trappings stored upward
cannot remove his presence, here.

for Vern Rutsala

BLACK STUDY

No one's been told
that black men
went first to the moon
the dark side
for dark brothers
without space ship
gravity complex
in our computer centers
government campuses
instant play and replay
white mice and pig-guineas
in concentric digital rows.

Someone has been
pulling brother's curls
into fancy barbed wire,
measuring his forelegs,
caressing his dense innards
into formaldehyde
pruning the jellied marrow:
a certain formula is appearing:
someone has been studying you.

We gave it life, mahogany hands,
loose in song;
we gave it to children
in paraffin—
our biology.
It grew lovely and indecent
into a female orchid,
and, of course, produced
children of its own.
We took it back again.

ON SABBATICAL

We're in Sistine Chapel,
thousands of cranes waiting to feed
our fancy American tongues.

The girl I stand next to
is from Poughkeepsie, New York.
Since I'm a head taller I tell

her the life of Italy
in another tongue.
She's amused, having camped on

each northern Alpian slope
or shared the common wine
or loved an Italian:

it is here I must
tell you of her flight
into heaven

or the dance
she did
getting out.

for Robert Wolterbeek

BLUES ALABAMA

She's blacker
than the night which holds
us in our communion
against the white picket fences.
There's clash in her eyes,
and she smiles whitely
to the tambourines.
There's a folk song audience
of rebels who lover
her mother into children,
and then the children,
and they're all in the roads
searching for the art
which makes singing
a blessing of hatred.

THE ANTS, THE INSECTS

The white ants come out
without their shells
blinded by sunlight
which explains their whiteness;
they are being assaulted
by other insects,
also without color,
though they are black, yellow and brown.
It is the Renaissance
and today,
slaveships and constellations,
technocrats and citizens—
they are the same ants,
the same insects on
wood or plastic,
all without style
or direction—
all looking for some
new place to go.

for Robert Chrisman

AMERICAN HISTORY

Those four black girls blown up
in that Alabama church
remind me of five hundred
middle passage blacks,
in a net, under water
in Charleston harbor
so *redcoats* wouldn't find them.
Can't find what you can't see
can you?

for John Callahan

WE ASSUME: ON THE DEATH OF OUR SON,
REUBEN MASAI HARPER

We assume
that in 28 hours,
lived in a collapsible isolette,
you learned to accept pure oxygen
as the natural sky;
the scant shallow breaths
that filled those hours
cannot, did not make you fly—
but dreams were there
like crooked palmprints on
the twin-thick windows of the nursery—
in the glands of your mother.

We assume
the sterile hands
drank chemicals in and out
from lungs opaque with mucus,
pumped your stomach,
eeked the bicarbonate in
crooked, green-winged veins,
out in a plastic mask;

A woman who'd lost her first son
consoled us with an angel gone ahead
to pray for our family—
gone into that sky
seeking oxygen,
gone into autopsy,
a fine brown powdered sugar,
a disposable cremation:

We assume
you did not know we loved you.

REUBEN, REUBEN

I reach from pain
to music great enough
to bring me back,
swollenhead, madness,
lovefruit, a pickle of hate
so sour my mouth twicked
up and would not sing;
there's nothing in the beat
to hold it in
melody and turn human skin;
a brown berry gone
to rot just two days on the branch;
we've lost a son,
the music, *jazz*, comes in.

DEATHWATCH

Twitching in the cactus
hospital gown, a loon
on hairpin wings,
she tells me how
her episiotomy
is perfectly sewn
and doesn't hurt
while she sits in a pile
of blood
which once cleaned
the placenta
my third son should be in.
She tells me how early
he is, and how strong,
like his father,
and long, like a black-
stemmed Easter rose
in a white hand.

Just under five pounds
you lie there, a collapsed
balloon doll, burst in your
fifteenth hour, with the face
of your black father,
his fingers, his toes,
and eight voodoo
adrenalin holes in
your pinwheeled hair-lined
chest; you witness
your parents sign the autopsy
and disposal papers
shrunken to duplicate

in black ink
on white paper
like the country
you were born in,
unreal, asleep,
silent, almost alive.

This is a dedication
to our memory
of three sons—
two dead, one alive—
a reminder of a letter
to DuBois
from a student
at Cornell—on behalf
of his whole history class.
The class is confronted
with a question,
and no one—
not even the professor—
is sure of the answer:
"Will you please tell us
whether or not it is true
that negroes
are not able to cry?"

America needs a killing.
America needs a killing.
Survivors will be human.

ANOTHER SEASON

She tells me she feels
flutters for the fourth time
in three years.

Rain and wind scuff
four inches of leaves
to a porch full of toys—

our first son's—
another and another
season come on

and a child climbs
up her womb
towards her belly.

I've written poems
intentionally
to wash off

Reuben, Michael;
Reuben, Michael
gone on.

Now I write this poem,
early, feeling the movement
in the belly go on.

for Shirl

NIGHTMARES AGAIN

Nightmares again:
the uterus contracts,
squeezed walnut or prune;
the breasts ooze
useless milk
in ache of lost child
out of her body
out of the world
in a fine powdered dust.
Birth wreaks in her teeth,
wavering each night
to its endless, gnashing conclusion.
Nightmares again:
Nightmares again.

NEW SEASON

My woman has picked
all the leaves,
rolled her hands into locks,
gone into the woods
where I have taught her
the language of these wood leaves,
and the red sand plum trees.
It is a digest
of my taking these leaves with hunger;
it is love she understands.
From my own wooden smell
she has shed her raisin skin
and come back
sweetened into brilliant music:
Her song is our new season.

                              for Shirl

69

AFTER THE OPERATIONS

Strung up
in three major
explorations
your stomach is
American roadwork;
Indian brown,
strawberry marks,
and twenty-six
pills a day;
medical workings
upon you.

Now your daughter
reminds me
of Eskimo art
where a man
liberates the form
which lies within
his own glacial
craftsmanship
and makes his woman.
And you're her mother.
If I credit
her I credit you
with workmanship
all your own—
nerve endings
you've passed on:
in those scars
are foottracks of our love.

for Ruth

Christmas eve and no presents;
the snow's in the mountains;
the fat saint hasn't gotten
his witless teamwork from ski
trails and mushroomed mountaintops;
the lake water is truly sky-blue—
everybody's waiting for dark.
The minstrels take the lawns
to attract the skyflies
coming at midnight, in flight,
red-suited saint, with his whip
and his sack full of toys:
it can't be Halloween.

My backyard is covered with snow;
eight rabbits in reins settle their
cottontail feet in the molasses earth
and begin their whimsical dancing,
a figure-eight cycle
of rhythm and blues.

I see rose-thorned tambourines: see
that green honey-dewed fruit,
see the white sheets and pillow cases;
see that grayhaired black story-teller
on the porch swing;
even you are a believer.

MOLASSES AND THE THREE WITCHES

Inside out, the police announce
there's a riot—on CBS—
it's a barnfire.
Firemen and police
Ball-eye into the squares:
this is the first barnfire
in history.
Roll 'em:
Lady says she saw
the first keg of molasses
in a gunny sack
on a huge black's back;
a black rose bush
on his big-eared helper;
flour and grits
in a pelt as soft as snow—
all gone up in the smoke
of the last spiritual
of Bre'rs Bear,
Rabbit, Fox—
the black trinity:
I will not go quietly—
I will not go quietly—
I will not go quietly—

AFTERMATH

Blacks all dead
in the streets;
the guerrillas run
white sympathizers in,
out of the hills;
the city streets are
brush fires of the last
lovely battle.
There were those who did
not believe, on both sides,
in the fury of those last
night's human fires;
ready-made armies
hunt even the freeways.
Now the flames suck
kerosened human flesh
as the hostages loom,
military twigs
in this medicinal barbecue:
the country, finally, is white with snow.

DEAR JOHN, DEAR COLTRANE

a love supreme, a love supreme
a love supreme, a love supreme

Sex fingers toes
in the marketplace
near your father's church
in Hamlet, North Carolina—
witness to this love
in this calm fallow
of these minds,
there is no substitute for pain:
genitals gone or going,
seed burned out,
you tuck the roots in the earth,
turn back, and move
by river through the swamps,
singing: *a love supreme, a love supreme*;
what does it all mean?
Loss, so great each black
woman expects your failure
in mute change, the seed gone.
You plod up into the electric city—
your song now crystal and
the blues. You pick up the horn
with some will and blow
into the freezing night:
a love supreme, a love supreme—

Dawn comes and you cook
up the thick sin 'tween
impotence and death, fuel
the tenor sax cannibal
heart, genitals and sweat
that makes you clean—
a love supreme, a love supreme—

Why you so black?
cause I am
why you so funky?
cause I am
why you so black?
cause I am
why you so sweet?
cause I am
why you so black?
cause I am
a love supreme, a love supreme:

So sick
you couldn't play *Naima*,
so flat we ached
for song you'd concealed
with your own blood,
your diseased liver gave
out its purity,
the inflated heart
pumps out, the tenor kiss,
tenor love:
a love supreme, a love supreme—
a love supreme, a love supreme—

A MOTHER SPEAKS:

THE ALGIERS MOTEL INCIDENT, DETROIT

It's too dark to see black
in the windows of Woodward
or Virginia Park.
The undertaker
pushed his body back
into place
with plastic and gum
but it wouldn't
hold water.
When I looked
for marks
or lineament
or fine stitching
I was led away
without seeing
this plastic
face they'd built
that was not my son's.
They tied the eye
torn out
by shotgun
into place
and his shattered
arm cut away
with his buttocks
that remained.
My son's gone
by white hands
though he said
to his last word—
"Oh I'm so sorry,
officer, I broke your gun."

MR. P. C.

Paul Laurence Dunbar Chambers—
what a long history
of perfection, bass man,
those swollen solos
on Miles's Standard
teachings—"Blues"
dum, dum, dum, dum, dum.

If Mingus is monster
star, you are his
private brother, so soft
baby, so beauteous
in your shuffling,
how many soundful
dysplexia did you do it
over and over and over
do it to everybody's gutstrings
listening as flat out,
Jim, as harpheart and bone—
What a long history
Paul Laurence Dunbar Chambers,
and your namesakes,
in the chambers.

A FLAT RIDE

On a flat ride
to Oakland airport
my twin black star
sweeps the airways
with a kerosened rag
mop, and a silver smile,
fire all around us;
the beauteous smoke
we've inhaled
isn't blooming on radio
K-SOL and *K-JAZ* who've
commenced to crop into
black panthers
white men in unmarked
cars and fine co-eds
from Cal.

For another $100
I'll remake Berkeley
into the funky pool
hall it is
glimmering with contracts
newly constructed
in blotting ghetto fowl,
heavies from next door,
baby, to go upward
into a concrete
jooging machine.

Now Oakland sits
on a beefcake window
of an American-made

super jet for Holland,
my fellow Americans,
you who can transform
every black thing into
guitar, speed and handicraft—
what will you do to us
over the Arctic circle
like a slick Indian
reservation
collapsing on our children
to be born children again?

for Harry Hobbs

GAILGONE

Sorry you are dead
wondrously the clear answers
fill into our eyes—
candid mucous membranes
and our love for you
at your going:
hear us in our anatomy lessons.
We think you easier
having put all answers down,
the bones of your face
clearly of smoke,
white, sulphrous, dry;
sorry you are dead
we milk our physical goodbyes.

for Gail Jackson

ON CIVIL DISORDERS

You know you can't
tell these people anything.
Gone with the wind, baby.
What's white racism, boss?
Guess who's coming to dinner?
They're burning some stores
and their own homes.
What is police brutality, boss?
What is wrong with American
institutions, anyway?
Hear of the protestant ethic?
Martin, Martin's praying.
Who's overcoming whom:
You can't tell
these people anything.
What are invisible men?
Why should we burn up
that constitution
and pass out
them fat *care* packages
full of pink-titted
white girls (whose daughters?)
and them golden cadillacs.
We must get
our posse together
at once, at once:
niggers are coming.

The pit-vipers are asleep
having wreathed through
each bullet-hole memory
qued by the new religion:
we are now a black establishment
in our love for you.

It is astonishing
how four years gashed
wider chasms in our story
in our mayflower
and your famous postcard
to PLAYBOY—
Xmas card to follow:
"Happiness by any means necessary."

We've placed some Malcolmesque
soul brothers near the soul kits;
who walks the schizophrenic line?
what is terror but a black orchid,
a white lightnin' bouquet:
St. Malcolm at the Oracle:
A-um-ni-pad-me-hum:
Another brother gone.

BARRICADES

Barricades hammered into place,
the beams stake out
in broad daylight
to avert nothing
they've taken; the old second
floor where they write the checks,
synchronize the grades,
or type in correct places
a stream data prognosis
is taken in the night;
the magpies are around, around
the corporate desk.

The blacks are studying
the records kept,
memorizing the numbers,
tallying the secret exits,
remembering the names,
the window pipes, outside,
for the way down.

They've gotten up there
with Frederick Douglass
in a six hour duel
with the overseers,
the first confrontation
to his own man;
DuBois in Atlanta
looking at the fingers
toes of meat market Sam;
and Malcolm in his first

act crumbling his prison
and the bullet proof glass.

Someone is having a familiar
vision of the black-white syndrome
in the academic halls;
in the cigar smoke
one hears the full-bull
rhesis rhetoric
and the black Christmas
in the halls of ivy:
the barricades come down—

for Ronnie Herndon

ODE TO TENOCHTITLAN

Socks and gloves
the medal of honor
ablaze in twin fists
of two men
blackened in the imperial fires;
they stand before Coltrane
in their beauty,
the new emblem—
ANOTHER BROTHER GONE—
a style so resilient
and chromatic the pure
reeds of their bodies
bulge through metric
distances in their
special rhythms.
The impossible bowels
of round forms
digest the air
of the television
cameras in
a new vision
now on Olympus;
moon-children,
Gemini, the black stopwatch.

We have heard
the cries
bend the index,
the word-form
plumed black,
the traditional images.
Who can understand

having thought life
was somehow,
transmuted and cleansed
transistored
into a machine.

In the heats,
in the instant replays,
amidst the circuits
of brain waves
come back into
rhythm with a fisted
victory in another
game, a new
current, a new
exchange, a new
vision:
as a twin black spirit,
brother's come on home.

for Tommy Smith & John Carlos

Another brother gone
another brother gone
another brother gone
another brother gone
another brother gone
another brother gone

Gray hair and puffed bellies
the stomach moves out
to its specialty—
floating children first,
without smiles
The Soviet Union
lays it out
on the consumers
starving
in the oil slick
whites of their eyes;
the Red Cross
bandages
the refugee
camps in a white
blockade:

another brother gone
another brother gone
another brother gone
another brother gone
another brother gone
another brother gone

Egyptian pilots
cash the American checks—

Lagos, old England,
Washington
are animal kingdoms
in the guts of war:
there is no war
that's not famine
members of the UN

Biafra is an eastern
community in revolt
across territorial lines
worked out with a European
compass: fathom the sectioning
off Biafra—

There is no famine
there is no genocide
only a community
in revolt, only
the refinement of oil
slicks, only a black
smell, sunken, aglow:

another brother gone
another brother gone
another brother gone
another brother gone
another brother gone
another brother gone

for Odinachi Nwosu

POETRY FROM ILLINOIS

History Is Your Own Heartbeat
Michael S. Harper (1971)

The Foreclosure
Richard Emil Braun (1972)

The Scrawny Sonnets and Other
Narratives
Robert Bagg (1973)

The Creation Frame
Phyllis Thompson (1973)

To All Appearances: Poems New
and Selected
Josephine Miles (1974)

Nightmare Begins Responsibility
Michael S. Harper (1975)

The Black Hawk Songs
Michael Borich (1975)

The Wichita Poems
Michael Van Walleghen (1975)

Cumberland Station
Dave Smith (1977)

Tracking
Virginia R. Terris (1977)

Poems of the Two Worlds
Frederick Morgan (1977)

Images of Kin: New and Selected
Poems
Michael S. Harper (1977)

On Earth as It Is
Dan Masterson (1978)

Riversongs
Michael Anania (1978)

Goshawk, Antelope
Dave Smith (1979)

Death Mother and Other Poems
Frederick Morgan (1979)

Local Men
James Whitehead (1979)

Coming to Terms
Josephine Miles (1979)

Searching the Drowned Man
Sydney Lea (1980)

With Akhmatova at the Black
Gates
Stephen Berg (1981)

More Trouble with the Obvious
Michael Van Walleghen (1981)

Dream Flights
Dave Smith (1981)

The American Book of the Dead
Jim Barnes (1982)

Northbook
Frederick Morgan (1982)

The Floating Candles
Sydney Lea (1982)

Collected Poems, 1930–83
Josephine Miles (1983)

The River Painter
Emily Grosholz (1984)

The Passion of the Right-Angled
Man
T. R. Hummer (1984)

Healing Song for the Inner Ear
Michael S. Harper (1984)

Dear John, Dear Coltrane
Michael S. Harper (1985)